# SATAN THE CREDIT HE IS DUE

**IT'S TIME TO TAKE SATAN SERIOUSLY**

*Dr. Bruce Becker*

Published by Straight Talk Books
P.O. Box 301, Milwaukee, WI 53201
800.661.3311 • timeofgrace.org

Copyright © 2018 Time of Grace Ministry

All rights reserved. This publication may not be copied, photocopied, reproduced, translated, or converted to any electronic or machine-readable form in whole or in part, except for brief quotations, without prior written approval from Time of Grace Ministry.

Scripture is taken from THE HOLY BIBLE, NEW INTERNATIONAL VERSION®. NIV®. Copyright © 1973, 1978, 1984, 2011 by Biblica, Inc.® Used by permission. All rights reserved worldwide.

Printed in the United States of America
ISBN: 978-1-949488-02-9

TIME OF GRACE *and* IT ALL STARTS NOW *are registered marks of Time of Grace Ministry.*

# Contents

Introduction ........................................................................... 5

Satan Is THE Evil One ........................................................ 7

Satan Is Your Number-One Enemy ............................. 14

Satan Will Attack You ..................................................... 18

Satan Wants to Scam You ............................................. 26

Satan Will Tempt You ..................................................... 39

Satan Will Accuse You ................................................... 46

Conclusion .......................................................................... 52

# Introduction

In October 2013, Supreme Court Justice Antonin Scalia did an interview with *New York Magazine*. The interview covered a wide range of topics. The topic that seemed to surprise Scalia's interviewer, Jennifer Senior, the most was what he said about the devil. After a brief dialogue on heaven and hell, Scalia leaned toward Senior and stage-whispered, "I even believe in the Devil." "You do?" Senior responded. "Of course! Yeah, he's a real person," Scalia replied.

Senior went on to ask Scalia if he had seen any evidence of the devil lately. Scalia responded, "You know, it is curious. In the Gospels, the Devil is doing all sorts of things. He's making pigs run off cliffs; he's possessing people and whatnot. And that doesn't happen very much anymore. . . . It's because he's smart."

Senior asked, "So what's he doing now?" Scalia replied, "What he's doing now is getting people not to believe in him or in God. He's much more successful that way."[1]

It appears that Satan is having success at getting people not to believe in him, even among Christians. In a 2009 survey, Barna Research discovered that only 35% of Christians in the United States believe that Satan is a real being.[2] That is both surprising and very disconcerting.

American theologian R. C. Sproul once wrote: "To underestimate Satan is to suffer from the pride that goes before destruction. To overestimate him is to grant him more honor and respect than he deserves."[3]

It appears that Satan isn't getting much respect these days. And he likes it that way.

The reason for writing this book is because a greater number of Christians today (let alone those who don't call Jesus their Lord) appear to be underestimating Satan and his deadly attacks. His attacks target not only Christians but all of humanity. He targets individuals and families. He influences the attitudes and actions of people on the street and in the workplace. He's set up shop in government agencies and has the ear of world leaders. We also find him lurking around individual churches and denominations to see what kind of trouble he can instigate.

We need to stop underestimating Satan and ignoring him. We need to understand better his motivation, his tactics, and his goals. He has us in his sights. Yet, at the same time, we don't need to fear him or cower from him. We can stand up against him. The New Testament writer James reminds us, **"Submit yourselves, then, to God. Resist the devil, and he will flee from you"** (James 4:7).

It's time to take Satan seriously and give him the credit he is due.

# Satan Is THE Evil One

There are different names and titles for Satan in the Bible. The most commonly occurring are "Satan" and "devil." *Satan* is a Hebrew word and *devil* is a Greek word. They both have similar meanings: "accuser," "adversary," "slanderer." The New Testament uses Satan and devil interchangeably. Another common name that the Bible uses for Satan is the evil one. It's a title that gives us insight into the nature of who he is.

Satan didn't start out as evil. Originally, he was created by God as a holy angel. Although we can't pinpoint the exact moment the angels were created, the psalmist talks about the fact that angels were created: **"Praise him, all his angels; praise him, all his heavenly hosts. Let them praise the name of the Lord, for at his command they were created"** (Psalm 148:2,5).

Then, in the New Testament, we learn how Satan and other angels went from good to bad. Peter tells us that **"God did not spare angels when they sinned"** (2 Peter 2:4). Simply put, Satan disobeyed God.

In his brief New Testament letter, Jude gives us a little bit more information: **"The angels who did not keep their positions of authority but abandoned their proper dwelling—these he has kept in darkness, bound with everlasting chains for judgment on the**

**great Day"** (Jude 6). This suggests that these angels were dissatisfied with their position among the heavenly host and in some way rebelled against God.

Perhaps the best clue as to what was at the heart of Satan's sin is found in 1 Timothy. The apostle Paul, in writing about the qualifications for spiritual leaders in the church, says, **"He must not be a recent convert, or he may become conceited and fall under the same judgment as the devil"** (1 Timothy 3:6). Conceit or pride seems to be the root cause for Satan going from good to bad. There is a lesson here for us to take note of. The sin of pride can have serious consequences.

The Old Testament gives us some additional insight into Satan and his fall. In Isaiah chapter 14, Isaiah is writing about an earthly king, the king of Babylon, and prophesies his future demise. But prophecies in the Bible sometimes speak about two different people or events at the same time (i.e., in Matthew 24, Jesus prophesies both the destruction of Jerusalem and the end of the world). In Isaiah 14:12-15, Isaiah seems to be speaking about Satan in his words directed at the king of Babylon:

> **"How you have fallen from heaven,**
>    **morning star, son of the dawn!**
> **You have been cast down to the earth,**
>    **you who once laid low the nations!**
> **You said in your heart,**
>    **'I will ascend to the heavens; I will raise my throne above the stars of God;**
> **I will sit enthroned on the mount of assembly,**

> **on the utmost heights of Mount Zaphon.**
> **I will ascend above the tops of the clouds;**
> **I will make myself like the Most High.'**
> **But you are brought down to the realm of the dead,**
> **to the depths of the pit."**

The phrase "morning star" in verse 12 is translated in the King James Bible, as well as other translations, as "Lucifer." It's another name for Satan.

These verses suggest that Satan wanted to make himself "like the Most High." This sounds eerily familiar to what Satan, disguised as a talking serpent, told Adam and Eve in the Garden of Eden: **"You will be like God, knowing good and evil"** (Genesis 3:5). It was a lie—a lie that Satan himself had once believed.

Another place in the Old Testament that may give us some insight into Satan's demise is in Ezekiel chapter 28. Here again the words are directed to a king, this time the king of Tyre. Yet Satan seems to be pictured as the real "king" behind the wicked attitudes and actions of the king of Tyre:

> **"You were the seal of perfection,**
> **full of wisdom and perfect in beauty.**
> **You were in Eden,**
> **the garden of God; . . .**
> **You were anointed as a guardian cherub,**
> **for so I ordained you.**
> **You were on the holy mount of God;**
> **you walked among the fiery stones.**
> **You were blameless in your ways**

> from the day you were created
> till wickedness was found in you.
> Through your widespread trade
> you were filled with violence,
> and you sinned.
> So I drove you in disgrace from the mount of God,
> and I expelled you, guardian cherub,
> from among the fiery stones.
> Your heart became proud
> on account of your beauty,
> and you corrupted your wisdom
> because of your splendor.
> So I threw you to the earth;
> I made a spectacle of you before kings"
> (verses 12-17).

Satan is described as a cherub—a guardian angel—in the Garden of Eden. He was declared guilty of having committed wickedness and violence. As a consequence, he was driven out of the presence of God.

Isaiah prophesied death and destruction for the king of Babylon because he was an evil, wicked, and brutal king. Ezekiel prophesied death and destruction for the king of Tyre because he considered himself to be a god and as wise as the true God. Both of these kings reflected the evil character of Satan himself.

**The nature of Satan's character is indeed evil.**

The nature of Satan's character is indeed evil. It is on display when he tries to convince us that evil is good and good is evil. Where we see evil in the world, we know that Satan is playing a role in it, either directly or indirectly. The Bible tells us that **"the whole world is under the control of the evil one"** (1 John 5:19).

Evil takes on many different forms. Some of the greatest evil is carried out by serial killers, school shooters, and terrorists. Just as horrendous are acts of genocide, human sex trafficking, aborting babies and selling their body parts, and human torture. But there are other kinds of evil that destroy lives as well—abusive power plays in marriages, the home, the workplace, in church, or within government; cyberbullying; nasty divorces; anonymously emailing death threats; or the exploitation of the elderly. These are just a few examples of evil in our world. The complete list is much longer.

> **He is both the face of evil in the world and the mastermind behind it.**

There is one more place in the Bible that gives some additional insight into Satan and his demons going from good to bad. We'll dig into it later when we consider Satan as a serpent-dragon.

Give Satan the credit he is due. He is both the face of evil in the world and the mastermind behind it.

Not a one of us is insulated from evil or the attacks of Satan. That's why Jesus taught us to pray in the Lord's Prayer, **"Lead us not into temptation, but deliver us from the evil one"** (Matthew 6:13). That's also why Jesus prayed to his heavenly Father, **"My prayer is not that you take them out of the world but that** you protect them from the evil one" (John 17:15).

The apostle Paul reminds us that the greatest struggle we will ever face in this world is the struggle against the evil one: **"Put on the full armor of God, so that you can take your stand against the devil's schemes. For our struggle is not against flesh and blood, but against the rulers, against the authorities, against the powers of this dark world and against the spiritual forces of evil in the heavenly realms. Therefore put on the full armor of God, so that when the day of evil comes, you may be able to stand your ground, and after you have done everything, to stand"** (Ephesians 6:11-13).

The way we resist the devil and his spiritual forces is by putting on the full armor of God. The "full armor" refers to a complete set of tools used in defensive or offensive armament. Paul compares the full set of armor in the first century with the spiritual tools we use to defend ourselves against the evil one:

> **The way we resist the evil one and his spiritual forces is by putting on the full armor of God.**

**"Stand firm then, with the belt of truth buckled around your waist, with the breastplate of righteousness in place, and with your feet fitted with the readiness that comes from the gospel of peace. In addition to all this, take up the shield of faith, with which you can extinguish all the flaming arrows of the evil one. Take the helmet of salvation and the sword of the Spirit, which is the word of God"** (Ephesians 6:14-17).

Arm yourselves each day with truth, righteousness, peace, faith, God's gift of salvation, and the Word of God in order to do battle with the evil one. When you do, you will be able to stand against him.

# Satan Is Your Number-One Enemy

In the year 1930, the city of Chicago declared Al Capone "Public Enemy Number One."

This was a phrase coined at the time to describe individuals whose activities were overtly criminal and extremely damaging to society.

Capone, who was also known by his nickname Scarface, was an American gangster and businessman. He lived during Prohibition and ran a multimillion-dollar Chicago operation in gambling, bootlegging, and prostitution. Capone was known for his brutal acts of violence, the worst of which was the St. Valentine's Day Massacre when he ordered the murder of seven rival gang leaders. It was this event that led the Chicago media to tag him with the moniker Public Enemy Number One.

A few years later, in 1934, the Federal Bureau of Investigation declared another gangster Public Enemy Number One. His name was John Dillinger. Dillinger was a notorious and brutal robber. From September 1933 until July 1934, he and his violent gang incited terror on the upper Midwest. They were responsible for killing ten men and wounding seven others. They robbed banks for money and police arsenals for weapons. They staged three jailbreaks and, in the process, killed a sheriff during one and wounded two guards in another one.

So who is the real Public Enemy Number One? Is it

Capone? Is it Dillinger? Neither. It is Satan. Capone and Dillinger were just his accomplices.

Jesus told a parable about a man who planted a field with seeds of wheat. But when everyone in his household was sleeping, an enemy came and sowed weeds among the wheat. After a few weeks, the wheat sprouted and began to grow. Heads of grain soon began to appear. About the same time the weeds also started to grow among the wheat. The servants of the landowner came to him concerned about where the weeds came from. He told the servants that an enemy had done it. The servants then asked if they should go out into the field and pull up the weeds. The landowner told them not to because, in the process, some of the wheat might also get uprooted. He went on to tell his servants that, at the end of the growing season, the harvesters would separate the weeds from the wheat. The wheat would be gathered into the barn, and the weeds would be bundled and burned.

**So who is the real Public Enemy Number One? It is Satan.**

Behind the everyday stories of Jesus' parables, there was always a deeper or hidden meaning. When asked for the meaning of it, Jesus explained the parable of the wheat and the weeds to his disciples: **"The one who sowed the good seed is the Son of Man. The field is the world, and the good seed stands for the people of the kingdom. The weeds are the people of the evil one, and the enemy who sows them is the devil. The harvest is the end of the age, and the harvesters are**

**angels. As the weeds are pulled up and burned in the fire, so it will be at the end of the age. The Son of Man will send out his angels, and they will weed out of his kingdom everything that causes sin and all who do evil. They will throw them into the blazing furnace, where there will be weeping and gnashing of teeth. Then the righteous will shine like the sun in the kingdom of their Father"** (Matthew 13:37-43).

There are several takeaways for us from Jesus' explanation of his parable. First, the obvious—Satan is an enemy. No, more than that. He is THE enemy, along with his supernatural army of demons. An enemy is someone who is actively and continuously hostile toward someone else. That describes Satan and his army perfectly.

Satan is the enemy of Jesus. That makes him the enemy of every follower of Jesus too. And, not only are Satan and the demons enemies we have to deal with directly; Satan also has his own human accomplices, and he plants them in and around our lives, like weeds among the wheat. They may live next door. They may be coworkers or schoolmates. They could be on your rec-league team or in your social circles. They could even be a family member or a fellow worshiper at church. This means that there is a trifecta of enemies with hostile designs on every Christian—Satan, his demons, and his accomplices in the world.

Do you know what the bad news is? Satan and his followers are not going away anytime soon. They will be in this world harassing followers of Jesus until the final judgment day. Only then will they be gathered by the holy angels and segregated to the eternal punishment that awaits them in hell.

Do you know what the good news is? Satan can't destroy us. His demons can't harm us. His followers can't hurt us. They can do none of these things as long as we remain in Jesus. The writer John assures us of this in one of his letters: **"The One who was born of God keeps them safe, and the evil one cannot harm them. We know that we are children of God, and that the whole world is under the control of the evil one. We know also that the Son of God has come and has given us understanding, so that we may know him who is true. And we are in him who is true by being in his Son Jesus Christ. He is the true God and eternal life"** (1 John 5:18-20).

> **Satan can't destroy us. His demons can't harm us as long as we remain in Jesus.**

Give Satan the credit he is due. He is our number-one enemy. But he can't harm us as God's children because the One born of God—Jesus—keeps us safe.

# Satan Will Attack You

**Lion**

When I was a kid in grade school, our family lived in northwest Wisconsin, about two hours east of Minneapolis/St. Paul, Minnesota. I remember a couple of family trips to the Twin Cities to go to the Como Park Zoo. My fondest memory was being able to ride (more like sit) on a Galápagos tortoise. Since these tortoises can live to be one hundred years old, maybe the one I rode is still there (not likely!).

Of course, when we went to the zoo, we had to see all the wild animals—including the lions, the king of the beasts. All of the big cats were in cages, and most of them could be found taking naps. Some would walk around their cages on their massive paws and occasionally open their huge mouths, revealing their sharp, pointed teeth. Even so, they seemed fairly harmless to a seven-year-old.

That was until a new wildlife program began airing on television. It was called *Mutual of Omaha's Wild Kingdom*. The show was a half-hour program that aired on Sundays on the NBC station (one of only four stations available on our black and white TV). Marlin Perkins was the host of the show along with his partner and sidekick, Jim Fowler. Each week Perkins and Fowler explored the wild kingdoms of the world.

After watching *Wild Kingdom*, a seven-year-old can gain a whole new respect for the big cats. In those days, producers didn't show the actual kill scene of a lion taking down a wildebeest, impala, or zebra. What they did show was a scene of the lion chasing its intended prey followed by a scene depicting a partially eaten carcass on the ground, with mama lion gnawing away at it along with her young cubs. But everyone understood what happened in between those two scenes. The lion killed its prey.

Lions aren't harmless. They are life-threateningly dangerous. Every year we hear a story or two of zookeepers who are mauled by the big cats or we learn of people ambushed by them in the safari parks of South Africa. With videos of such tragic events uploaded to YouTube, we don't just hear about these tragedies; we can see and experience their horror.

The apostle Peter compares Satan to a lion that prowls the earth looking for people to attack: **"Be alert and of sober mind. Your enemy the devil prowls around like a roaring lion looking for someone to devour"** (1 Peter 5:8). Just as a lion prowls around looking for prey, Satan looks for people he can target for a kill, you and me included.

> **Just as a lion prowls around looking for prey, Satan looks for people he can target for a kill.**

Give Satan the credit he is due. He is like a powerful, vicious lion that wants to kill you.

But then Peter goes on to say, **"Resist him, standing firm in the faith, because you know that the family of believers throughout the world is undergoing the same kind of sufferings"** (1 Peter 5:9).

Resist Satan because he can be resisted. We don't

have to surrender to his attacks. The defense against Satan the lion is standing firm on our faith foundation in Jesus.

**Serpent-Dragon**

When it comes to mythological creatures, dragons are among the most popular and the most fearsome. Tales about these large, serpentlike creatures span the world's cultures and have endured for centuries. Some dragons are depicted as having wings and the ability to fly. Some breathe fire. Other dragons, like those in eastern cultures, are typically represented as a four-legged serpentine creature. The earliest depicted dragons, primarily from ancient archeological sources in the Middle East, are like giant snakes.

One of the more well-known dragons within the last century is Smaug, described in J. R. R. Tolkien's novel the *Hobbit.* Smaug was a powerful dragon that had invaded the dwarf kingdom of Erebor because he greedily wanted the wealth that the dwarfs had stashed in a mountain. The story is about a small band of dwarfs and others traveling to the mountain to slay the dragon who had been guarding the treasure for 150 years.

In Tolkien's the *Lord of the Rings*, we read about other dragons that are ridden by the Ringwraiths in pursuit of Frodo Baggins and his companions. Dragons were common in Tolkien's writings. Even more recently are the dragons that appear in J. K. Rowling's Harry Potter books. One of the dragon occurrences was when Harry did battle with the Hungarian Horntail during the Triwizard Tournament in *Harry Potter and the Goblet of Fire*.

Whether the source of information is thousands of years old or books written in the last few decades, dragons have long been a part of many different cultures' oral and written folklore.

There is, however, one dragon, a serpent-dragon, that isn't a fantasy tale.

We meet this serpent-dragon for the first time in the opening chapters of Genesis, where this creature is simply referred to as a "serpent." To know with certainty that this serpent is Satan (he's never called that in Genesis), we look to Revelation for insight: **"I saw an angel coming down out of heaven, having the key to the Abyss and holding in his hand a great chain. He seized the dragon, that ancient serpent, who is the devil, or Satan . . ."** (20:1,2). The serpent-dragon that confronted Eve and Adam in the Garden of Eden was Satan, disguised as a snake.

In the Garden of Eden, Satan came to Eve and asked her, **"Did God really say, 'You must not eat from any tree in the garden'?"** (Genesis 3:1). Satan first sowed seeds of doubt. Eve replied by telling Satan that if they ate from the tree in the middle of the garden (the tree of the knowledge of good and evil), they would die. **"'You will not certainly die,' the serpent said to the woman. 'For God knows that when you eat from it your eyes will be opened, and you will be like God,**

> **The serpent-dragon was Satan, disguised as a snake.**

**knowing good and evil'"** (Genesis 3:4,5). Satan lied.

When Adam and Eve ate of the forbidden fruit, their eyes were indeed opened, but not to see something good. Their eyes were opened to see their disobedience to God. Now things would never be the same. They lost their perfect world. They lost their perfect life. They lost their perfect relationship with their Creator, each other, and all of God's creation. Now life would be hard. It would be filled with pain and conflict. And worst of all, life would eventually end in death.

> **Satan achieved what he set out to do.**

Satan achieved what he set out to do. Give him the credit he is due. Satan played the part of a serpent perfectly. You see, serpent-dragons want only one thing for their potential victims. They want to see their victims die.

In addition to Genesis chapter 3 and Revelation chapter 20, we meet this serpent-dragon one more time in the 12th chapter of Revelation. This chapter marks the beginning of the fourth vision revealed by God to the apostle John, who had been banished to the island of Patmos. The fourth vision is actually a series of seven individual visions.

The chapter begins, **"A great sign appeared in heaven: a woman clothed with the sun, with the moon under her feet and a crown of twelve stars on her head. She was pregnant and cried out in pain as she was about to give birth"** (verses 1,2). A few verses later, we learn that the woman **"gave birth to a son, a male child, who 'will rule all the nations with an iron**

**scepter.' And her child was snatched up to God and to his throne"** (verse 5).

We can determine who this male child is by looking to other places in Scripture. It's Jesus, the Son of God. King David, writing in Psalm 2, prophesied that the coming Savior would **"rule his enemies with an iron scepter"** (verse 9). So does that mean that the woman is Mary, Jesus' mother? We might think so until we read how this woman is described throughout the chapter. Without going into a lot of explanatory detail, the woman is symbolic of the church in the New Testament age. The last verse of the chapter suggests this: **"Then the dragon was enraged at the woman and went off to wage war against the rest of her offspring—those who keep God's commands and hold fast their testimony about Jesus"** (Revelation 12:17). The woman represents the sum total of all Christ followers.

But we haven't yet talked about the dragon. Let's go back to verses 3 and 4 to hear it described: **"Then another sign appeared in heaven: an enormous red dragon with seven heads and ten horns and seven crowns on its heads. Its tail swept a third of the stars out of the sky and flung them to the earth. The dragon stood in front of the woman who was about to give birth, so that it might devour her child the moment he was born."**

Wow, what a terrifying image! This enormous red dragon stood in front of the woman who was about to give birth for the purpose of devouring the child—who we know as Jesus—the moment he was born. Remember, dragons want just one thing for their potential victims—they want them to die.

After reading these words, we can't help but think of King Herod's order to kill all the baby boys in Bethlehem at the time of Jesus' birth. The wise men from the East had come looking for the newborn King whose star they had seen. They asked Herod where he could be found. This was disturbing news for Herod. There was a rival king living in the country!? Herod inquired of the Jewish religious leaders where this King was to be born. They told him that he was to be born in Bethlehem. Herod then told the wise men to let him know where this child could be found so he could go and worship him too. Not! Herod wanted to find him so he could kill him. Do you think Satan had anything to do with King Herod's massacre order of the Bethlehem boys? You can count on it.

Included in the vision in Revelation chapter 12 is one more indication of what took place after Satan rebelled against God after the creation of the heavenly host: **"Then war broke out in heaven. Michael and his angels fought against the dragon, and the dragon and his angels fought back. But he was not strong enough, and they lost their place in heaven. The great dragon was hurled down—that ancient serpent called the devil, or Satan, who leads the whole world astray. He was hurled to the earth, and his angels with him"** (verses 7-9).

When Satan rebelled, a spiritual war broke out with Satan and the evil angels (the one-third described as being swept out of the sky by the dragon) on one side and Michael and the holy angels on the other. Michael was and still is the archangel in charge of God's army of heavenly angels. Satan and the demons lost that war. They lost their place in heaven and were hurled out to the earth where he now roams.

Before you throw your hands up in hopelessness because the dragon is roaming around the earth in search of victims like you and me, hear this assurance from our God: **"Then I heard a loud voice in heaven say: 'Now have come the salvation and the power and the kingdom of our God, and the authority of his Messiah. For the accuser of our brothers and sisters, who accuses them before our God day and night, has been hurled down. They triumphed over him by the blood of the Lamb and by the word of their testimony; they did not love their lives so much as to shrink from death. Therefore rejoice, you heavens and you who dwell in them!'"** (Revelation 12:10-12).

Satan and his evil band have been defeated by the blood of the Lamb. Jesus the Messiah has rescued us. The kingdom of our God will always endure. Satan the serpent-dragon will try to destroy **"those who keep God's commands and hold fast their testimony about Jesus"** (Revelation 12:17). But he won't be successful because Jesus has triumphed over him.

> **But he won't be successful because Jesus has triumphed over him.**

Give Satan the credit he is due. He is a deadly serpent-dragon looking for victims. But give our God the glory he is due. Through Jesus he has rescued us from Satan and defends us against him.

# Satan Wants to Scam You

When I was a senior in college, I directed a theatrical production of Shakespeare's *A Midsummer Night's Dream*. The play is one of Shakespeare's comedies and features as a leading character a household sprite named Puck. In Elizabethan folklore, Puck (aka Robin Goodfellow) is a mischievous, hobgoblin fairy.

In this magical play, Shakespeare uses the character of Puck to serve as the court jester to Oberon, who is the king of the fairies. When he isn't doing his jester job, Puck is known for playing annoying pranks on unsuspecting humans. In one scene in the play, Puck turns the head of Nick Bottom, a weaver by trade, into that of a donkey and then causes Queen Titania to fall in love with the donkey-headed Bottom.

Puck is also known to "help" people with their chores by ruining vats of ale or spoiling freshly made butter. He has the ability to zip around the globe (in less than an hour) to find special flowers so King Oberon can make his magical love potion. Puck is especially fond of shape-shifting. He boasts of pretending to be a stool and then disappearing just as some lady is about to sit on it. Ha! Puck is a mischievous sprite who can make a mess of people's lives with his pranks. At other times, his good-natured side shows through as he manipulates events to have things turn out just fine so that people can live happily ever after.

The character of Puck seems to have a few characteristics in common with those of Satan—so-called "helping" people, speed of traveling the globe, deceiving people, and making a mess of people's lives. But Puck is a fictional character in an Elizabethan play. Satan, on the other hand, is real. Unlike Puck, he doesn't have a good-natured side, and he doesn't make things turn out in the end. Satan is a deceiver. He is a liar. He is a masquerader.

> **Satan is a deceiver. He is a liar. He is a masquerader.**

### Deceiver

When it comes to deceiving human beings, there is no one more skilled than Satan. We saw evidence of that in the Garden of Eden in how Satan deceived Adam and Eve into thinking that they could be like God. All they had to do was sample the fruit from the tree of the knowledge of good and evil.

Thousands of years later, in one of his letters that he wrote to the church in Corinth, the apostle Paul expresses his serious concern that the Corinthians would be deceived as Eve was: **"But I am afraid that just as Eve was deceived by the serpent's cunning, your minds may somehow be led astray from your sincere and pure devotion to Christ"** (2 Corinthians 11:3). Paul's words are a reminder of what doesn't change when it comes to Satan—once a deceiver, always a deceiver.

With Adam and Eve being the only two human beings on the earth at the time the first sin occurred, Satan was personally involved in carrying out the deception. As time went on, however, Satan began amassing his own followers and using willing human accomplices to do his deceiving.

There are many examples of this in the Bible. One well-known example (Hollywood even made an award-winning movie about it) is when God's Old Testament people, the nation of Israel, were enslaved in Egypt about 1500 B.C. God decided that it was time to lead his people out of Egypt. So God called upon the 80-year-old Moses and his 83-year-old brother, Aaron, to implement his plan.

The problem Moses and Aaron faced was that the pharaoh of Egypt wasn't willing to let millions of slave laborers leave the country. So God told Moses and Aaron to perform a series of miracles in the presence of the pharaoh. The first miracle involved Aaron throwing his staff down on the ground in front of the pharaoh. When he did, his staff became a snake. Not to be outdone, Pharaoh summoned his magicians and they were able to do the same with their "secret arts." Their staffs became snakes as well. Here we have an important contrast. God was the source of power in Aaron's miracle. Satan was the source of power in the magicians' miracle.

Despite the miracle, Pharaoh remained unwilling to let God's people leave Egypt, so Moses and Aaron performed a second miracle. God told them to stretch Aaron's staff over the Nile River, and it became blood; killing all the fish and making it unfit for either animals or people to drink it. Pharaoh's magicians used their satanic arts and did the same. Blood was everywhere, but it didn't change Pharaoh's unwillingness to let God's people go.

For the third miracle, God called up frogs out of the Nile River to invade all the spaces where people lived, even Pharaoh's palace, his kitchen, and even hopping on Pharaoh's bed in his bedroom. Ugh! But again, the magicians were able to mirror the miracle, and they produced their own frogs. Despite the invasion of the frogs, Pharaoh's heart remained unchanged.

It wasn't until the fourth miracle, when God sent a gazillion gnats, that the magicians weren't able to duplicate the miracle. **"When the magicians tried to produce gnats by their secret arts, they could not. Since the gnats were on people and animals everywhere, the magicians said to Pharaoh, 'This is the finger of God'"** (Exodus 8:18,19). Satan has great power, but it is limited. Satan can do miracles, but they are limited. Satan is powerful, but God is infinitely more powerful.

> Satan is powerful, but God is infinitely more powerful.

Today, Satan's accomplices don't turn rivers into blood streams. However, they still use their power to lead people astray with the allure of events existing outside the laws of nature. There is (and always has been) a fascination in our culture with the supernatural.

In 2005 a new television series entitled *Supernatural* debuted on the WB network. The series can be described as a dark fantasy tale. The story line involves two brothers, Sam and Dean Winchester, who hunt mysterious and demonic creatures. The plot is complicated with the haunting memories of their mother whom they lost to a supernatural force and a father who raised them to hunt the creatures of the dark.

The pilot program launched with more than five million viewers tuning in. In the fall of 2018, *Supernatural* began its 14th season. More than two million viewers continue to watch the program each week. The series has developed a cultlike following.

People tend to be intrigued with what they can't explain. Beyond television programs and the endless stream of new movies at the box office that have a supernatural theme, there is a personal intrigue with knowing the future and things unknown. Psychic readings, Tarot cards, and palm reading are touted as giving you a glimpse into your own future, good or bad. Astrology and horoscopes claim to predict your future based upon when you were born and whether your sign is Pisces, Libra, Sagittarius, or whatever. Then there are various iterations of divination that call upon Satan's power to learn secret information. Probably the most explicit expressions of the supernatural's dark side are the overt practices of witchcraft and the gathering of Satan followers into Wiccan covens.

> **Satan's goal is to deceive people and keep them from knowing Christ.**

Satan's goal with this fascination with the supernatural is to deceive people and keep them from knowing Christ. The apostle Paul sums it up well: **"The god of this age has blinded the minds of unbelievers, so that they cannot see the light of the gospel that displays the glory of Christ, who is the image of God"** (2 Corinthians 4:4).

Satan hides what's true. He keeps people from seeing the treasure of the gospel of Jesus. He lets people see facts and convincing evidence and even miracles. He entices with glimpses into the supernatural and things unknown. He distracts and deceives through a show of his power—all with the goal of keeping Christ hidden. Give Satan the credit he is due. He is a deceiver and, sadly, has blinded the minds of many.

Because of—and only because of—the grace of God, we don't live our lives with minds blinded to who Jesus is and what he has done for us. The Holy Spirit, working in our hearts, has removed the blindfold of unbelief so that we can see Jesus with eyes of faith. Jesus now lives in our hearts. Satan cannot deceive us any longer. But he would like to. He would like nothing better than to put a blindfold back on you and me and lead us away from Christ. For that reason, we need to stay closely connected with Jesus and the timeless truths of his Word.

Here is a Bible verse that's worth carrying around in your heart. It's a comforting reminder for all the times Satan or his accomplices show up to deceive you: **"You, dear children, are from God and have overcome them, because the one who is in you is greater than the one who is in the world"** (1 John 4:4).

**Liar**

Sometimes Satan tries to scam us by deceiving us and hiding the truth from us. Other times he just lies.

In the Garden of Eden, Satan suggested to Eve that she eat from the tree of the knowledge of good and evil, the only tree God said not to eat from. Satan scammed Eve with two back-to-back lies. The first lie was totally untrue. The second one was a half-lie. Satan promised Eve, **"You will not certainly die"** and **"You will be like God, knowing good and evil"** (Genesis 3:4,5). The truth was that if they ate the forbidden fruit, they would indeed die and that, although they would know good and evil, they would not be like God. Satan lied.

There is no clearer evidence in the Bible of "Satan = Liar" than what Jesus once said. During his ministry, Jesus was frequently confronted by the Jewish religious leaders. They did not accept Jesus as being sent from God, and they opposed him vigorously. On one occasion, in a dialogue about who the true children of God are, Jesus told the religious leaders that if God was their Father, they would love and follow him as God's Son. They rejected Jesus' assertion. As a result, Jesus denounced the religious leaders as being followers of Satan rather than followers of God:

**"You belong to your father, the devil, and you want to carry out your father's desires. He was a murderer from the beginning, not holding to the truth, for there is no truth in him. When he lies, he speaks his native language, for he is a liar and the father of lies"** (John 8:44).

Jesus had harsh condemnation both for Satan and for the religious leaders. Jesus condemned Satan for being a liar. Jesus condemned the religious leaders for swallowing Satan's lies hook, line, and sinker and for participating in Satan's desire to oppose and resist Jesus and God's timeless truth about him.

Jesus had firsthand experience with Satan's lies. In the next chapter, we'll take a look at Satan's temptation of Jesus in the wilderness and how he used lies and half-lies to try to lead Jesus to sin against his heavenly Father. (Spoiler alert! Satan was not successful!)

Do you know any habitual liars? If you do, it's best to stay away from them. Once lying is a part of a person's character, one lie leads to another and another and another. Lying also gets easier the more one does it. One of the sinister aspects of lying is that it's contagious. Like a deadly virus, exposure to habitual liars puts us at risk for infection in our own character that can result in serious spiritual harm. Stay away from habitual liars so that you don't become one of them.

**Don't let Satan anywhere near you with his lies.**

Even more so, don't let Satan anywhere near you with his lies. He wants to infect you so that you become as poisoned as he is. In the book of Acts, we read a story about a husband and wife couple who let Satan worm his way into their hearts. Their names were Ananias and Sapphira.

In Acts chapter 4, we learn about a grace-filled practice within the early church. God's people lived their faith by willingly and gladly sharing their possessions with others: **"All the believers were one in heart and mind. No one claimed that any of their possessions was their own, but they shared everything they had"** (Acts 4:32). People would sell parcels of land or houses and would give the proceeds to the apostles for others to benefit from. The result of this was that there weren't any needy persons within their community of believers.

One person who gave such a gift was a man named Joseph. He was from Cyprus, an island in the northeast corner of the Mediterranean Sea. Joseph is probably better known by a nickname—Barnabas—which means "son of encouragement." Barnabas sold a field that he owned and gave it to the apostles (Acts 4:36,37).

Then we learn that **"Ananias, together with his wife Sapphira, also sold a piece of property. With his wife's full knowledge he kept back part of the money for himself, but brought the rest and put it at the apostles' feet"** (Acts 5:1,2). There was nothing wrong with the couple only giving a portion of the proceeds. The problem was that they lied about it:

**"Then Peter said, 'Ananias, how is it that Satan has so filled your heart that you have lied to the Holy Spirit and have kept for yourself some of the money you received for the land? Didn't it belong to you before it was sold? And after it was sold, wasn't the money at your disposal? What made you think of doing such a thing? You have not lied just to human beings but to God'"** (Acts 5:3,4).

Ananias and Sapphira allowed Satan into their hearts and, once there, he led them to lie, not just to their community but to God himself. That day, because of their lie, God ended both Ananias' and Sapphira's lives on this earth.

The apostle John warns us: **"The one who does what is sinful is of the devil, because the devil has been sinning from the beginning."** And then John immediately follows his warning with this assurance: **"The reason the Son of God appeared was to destroy the devil's work"** (1 John 3:8). Jesus lived and died to set us free from the liar, Satan.

Give Satan the credit he is due. He is a master liar and will do whatever he can to get you and me to be one too. Thankfully, Jesus came to destroy the work of Satan and, when we remain connected to Jesus, we are able to resist his lies.

> **Jesus lived and died to set us free from the liar, Satan.**

### Masquerader

There is something enjoyable about dressing up in a costume and pretending to be something you're not. At Halloween kids (as well as adults) masquerade as their favorite superheroes, movie characters, animals, or make-believe monsters. The masqueraders then go door-to-door in their neighborhoods in search of treats. The wearing of costumes is intended to be fun for those standing on both sides of the front door.

Every year in countries around the world, "Carnival" celebrations are held between the Christian festivals of Epiphany (January 6) and Ash Wednesday. In the United States, the celebration is most often known as Mardi Gras. These celebrations around the world almost always involve the use of elaborate costumes and masks worn by the participants. The masquerade costume hides who a person really is and allows the person to be someone he or she is not.

Satan is a masquerader. He wakes up every morning and gets dressed in a different masquerade costume. Satan's accomplices in the world do the same. The apostle Paul wrote to the believers living in Corinth, warning them about people who were pretending to be teachers and apostles of Christ: **"For such people are false apostles, deceitful workers, masquerading as apostles of Christ. And no wonder, for Satan himself masquerades as an angel of light. It is not surprising, then, if his servants masquerade as servants of righteousness"** (2 Corinthians 11:13-15).

Satan was originally created to be an angel of light, a "morning star" (Isaiah 14:12), so he knows what the characteristics of an angel of light are and can masquerade as one. So how do we know if it is a real angel of light or Satan pretending to be one? Satan's accomplices masquerade as God's prophets, teachers, and Christ followers. How do we know if we are listening to a true prophet or teacher or a fake one? Jesus shows us how to determine it: **"Watch out for false prophets. They come to you in sheep's clothing, but inwardly they are ferocious wolves. By their fruit you will recognize them. Do people pick grapes from thornbushes, or figs from thistles? Likewise, every good tree bears good fruit, but a bad tree bears bad fruit. A good tree cannot bear bad fruit, and a bad tree cannot bear good fruit. Every tree that does not bear good fruit is cut down and thrown into the fire. Thus, by their fruit you will recognize them"** (Matthew 7:15-20).

We need to be on full-time lookout because Satan offers appealing counterfeits of God's truth. They can come in the form of false religions with their counterfeit teachings (i.e., the Quran, the central religious text of Islam; or the Book of Mormon and Doctrines and Covenants, two texts of the Church of Jesus Christ of Latter-Day Saints).

Satan's counterfeits can also come in the form of different philosophies and opinions. Satan has a stash of philosophical "isms" at his disposal that he uses as masquerades for truth (evolutionism, intellectualism, determinism, dualism, fatalism, naturalism, hedonism, etc.). One source lists 234 different philosophical isms, all counterfeit teachings to the Bible. Although we might not believe any of these isms in full, Satan is interested in getting us to believe one or more of them at least in part.

We also need to be on full-time lookout because Satan isn't going to look anything like we think he looks. No red suit. No horns. No pitchfork in hand. If anything, he will look like an angel or another human being. False prophets don't look like false prophets either. Fake followers of Christ don't look like fake followers. They all look like the real deal. That's because they are masqueraders.

**We need to be on full-time lookout because Satan offers appealing counterfeits of God's truth.**

We can be scammed by Satan and his many accomplices if we only pay attention to what appearances are. We need to look beyond appearances to their motivations and the results that come from their teachings. As Jesus says, **"By their fruit you will recognize them"** (Matthew 7:20).

Give Satan the credit he is due. He is a master masquerader. But Satan can be exposed for who he really is when we shine the light of God's truth on him.

# Satan Will Tempt You

In 2004 Mel Gibson produced and released a riveting film entitled *Passion of the Christ.* The film told the story of Jesus' suffering and death at the end of his three-year ministry. One interesting facet of the film was Gibson's portrayal of Satan.

In the movie, Satan appears in the Garden of Gethsemane where Jesus is praying. Gibson took significant creative license here, because the Bible does not indicate that Satan tempted Jesus in the garden. However, what the scene does accurately represent is the intense struggle Jesus was facing in going through with his forthcoming arrest, trial, and agonizing crucifixion. What was even more of a struggle for Jesus is that on the cross he would be forsaken by God in order to pay the penalty for the world's sin. Although the Bible doesn't say that Satan was lurking in the Garden of Gethsemane, he definitely wanted Jesus not to carry out God's plan to redeem the world.

In the film, Satan is portrayed as a ghostly creature with indiscriminant features. As Jesus is praying intensely facedown on the ground, a snake comes slithering out from underneath Satan's robe. It approaches Jesus. When Jesus gets up from the ground with the snake poised to strike, Jesus raises his foot and crushes the snake's head. This scene in the film takes us back to the Garden of Eden where God told the serpent Satan after Adam and Eve disobeyed God, **"I will put enmity between you and the woman, and between your off-**

**spring and hers; he will crush your head, and you will strike his heal"** (Genesis 3:15). Again, this film scene is not recorded in the Bible, but it does symbolize the real struggle Jesus went through as well as Satan being crushed and defeated by the offspring of Eve, namely Jesus Christ, the Son of God.

The truth is that Satan didn't wait until the end of Jesus' ministry to tempt him. He did it at the very beginning. The temptation of Jesus by Satan took place immediately after Jesus was baptized by John the Baptist in the Jordan River. At Jesus' baptism the Father stated his approval of his Son, and the Holy Spirit descended on him in the form of a dove. Following his baptism, Jesus began his three-year ministry.

From the Jordan, Jesus was led into the wilderness by the Holy Spirit to be tempted by the devil. It's interesting that Matthew uses the word *devil* instead of *Satan*. The word *devil* has more of an emphasis on slandering or lying than does the title *Satan*. Lying is exactly the plan of attack Satan used to tempt Jesus.

> **Lying is exactly the plan of attack Satan used to tempt Jesus.**

For 40 days and nights, Jesus fasted in the wilderness. How God sustained him during these weeks of fasting, we aren't told. It's not surprising then that the very first temptation by Satan had to do with food: **"If you are the Son of God, tell these stones to become bread"** (Matthew 4:3). Is this déjà vu or what? In the Garden of Eden, in tempting Eve and Adam, Satan began by sowing seeds of doubt. Here again he did it with

Jesus. He also used food with Eve. He now used the lack of food to tempt Jesus. Jesus responded to this temptation by quoting the Word of God: **"Man shall not live on bread along, but on every word that comes from the mouth of God"** (Matthew 4:4). This temptation of Satan was aimed at producing distrust of his heavenly Father in the heart of Jesus.

For the second temptation, Satan took Jesus to the highest point of the temple in Jerusalem (even though a moment earlier they were in the wilderness!). There Satan told Jesus to jump off the temple because **"he will command his angels concerning you, and they will lift you up in their hands, so that you will not strike your foot against a stone"** (Matthew 4:6). Satan quoted Psalm 91:11,12 to suggest that Jesus take God at his word. Satan tempted Jesus to have a false trust in God's promises. Jesus responded to this temptation by again quoting Scripture: **"It is also written: 'Do not put the Lord your God to the test'"** (Matthew 4:7).

For the third temptation, Satan took Jesus to a high mountain and showed him all the kingdoms of the world. Satan offered all of these kingdoms to Jesus if he would bow down and worship Satan and, in the process, abandon God's personally costly plan to save the world. Satan lied. Satan couldn't honor his promise and never would. Jesus replied, **"Away from me, Satan! For it is written: 'Worship the Lord your God, and serve him only'"** (Matthew 4:10,11).

With each temptation, Satan tried to drive a wedge between Jesus and his heavenly Father. With each temptation, Jesus responded by using the sword of the

Spirit, which is the Word of God. Satan was unsuccessful in his temptation of the Christ. So now he focuses his efforts on tempting the followers of Christ. Satan will tempt you. He is lurking at the door of your heart. Don't let him in.

Satan has many temptations that he uses. He will tempt believers to be prideful just like he tempted King David: **"Satan rose up against Israel and incited David to take a census of Israel"** (1 Chronicles 21:1). King David and the Israelite army had previously experienced many military victories, especially against the neighboring Philistines. With this military success, Satan tempted David to take a census and determine how many men could handle a sword in all of Israel. At the coaching of Satan, David took his eyes off of the fact that God was the one who blessed Israel with military victories. David wasn't successful because of the size of his army. It was because God gave him the victories. Satan was at the door of David's heart, tempting him to be proud of "his accomplishments." Sadly, David opened the door and let him in.

Pride has many faces or disguises. It can be boasting about my own experiences or accomplishments. It can be putting others down to make me seem more important. It can be when I magnify the sins of others so that my sins don't seem so bad. Pride can show its ugly face when I refuse to accept correction or won't take responsibility for my own actions. Pride goes before the fall.

One of the ugliest faces of pride is thinking that I am a better Christian because "I'm more faithful to the truth of the Bible" or "I show more love to other people" or "I belong to a certain church or denomination." C. S. Lewis put it this way: "Whenever we find that our religious life is making us feel that we are good—above all, that we are better than someone else—I think we may be sure that we are being acted on, not by God, but by the devil."[4] Satan stands at the door of our hearts, tempting us with pride. Don't let him in.

**Satan stands at the door of our hearts, tempting us with pride. Don't let him in.**

Another temptation Satan uses is materialism. In comparison to the rest of the world, people who live in the United States live in luxury, but it seems we always want more, and it's usually just more "stuff." We need to realize that always wanting more is a way Satan uses to tempt us to be dissatisfied with what we have.

In 2013 *Forbes Magazine* had a story comparing wealth in the U.S. to other countries around the world. The research showed that the "U.S. has the highest living standard for the rich." And when it comes to America's poor, "the typical person in the bottom 5 percent of the American income distribution is still richer than *68 percent* of the world's inhabitants."[5]

That's incredible and illustrates just how blessed we are!

Wise King Solomon reminds us about the temptations of materialism: **"Whoever loves money never has enough; whoever loves wealth is never satisfied with their income"** (Ecclesiastes 5:10). Satan stands at the door of our hearts, tempting us with materialism. Don't let him in.

Pride and materialism are two of Satan's favorite temptations. At least they are when he comes hunting for me. The list of temptations that Satan uses is, however, endless. Satan tempts believers to:

- be spiritually lazy; disconnected from God's truth
- lie and/or stretch the truth
- engage in sexual sins
- be unforgiving toward others
- doubt God's promises
- feel sorry for ourselves
- abuse our bodies with food, drink, or other substances
- worry about our finances or future
- compromise our integrity
- love beauty, power, or money
- become bitter, resentful, or vengeful
- _____

    (Fill in the blank with the temptation Satan most often uses on you.)

C. S. Lewis had an interesting take on another strategy Satan uses to tempt us to disobey God: "He (the devil) always sends errors into the world in pairs—pairs of opposites. . . . He relies on your extra dislike of one to draw you gradually into the opposite one. But do not let us be fooled. We have to keep our eyes on the goal and go straight through between both errors"[6]

Has Satan ever used this strategy on you? He has on me.

Give Satan the credit he is due. He will use whatever temptations work best with each of us. He knows where we are vulnerable. He knows what works.

Since we can expect Satan to tempt us, **"Submit yourselves, then, to God. Resist the devil, and he will flee from you"** (James 4:7).

# Satan Will Accuse You

Like a skilled boxer, Satan has a one-two punch. His first punch is to tempt us to disobey God. His second punch is then to accuse us of having disobeyed God. That seems like a cruel tactic, but that's the way Satan operates. And like a skilled boxer, he doesn't just throw his pair of punches occasionally. He does it continuously.

As mentioned earlier, the word *Satan* literally means, "accuser." In the Old Testament's original Hebrew language, the word for *Satan* and the word for *accuser* use the very same letters of the alphabet. Accuser is who Satan is and what he does.

One of the saddest examples of Satan's one-two punch is the story of Judas Iscariot. Judas, one of Jesus' 12 disciples, loved money and was a thief. So it is no surprise that Satan used Judas' weakness as the basis for his temptation: **"Now the Festival of Unleavened Bread, called the Passover, was approaching, and the chief priests and the teachers of the law were looking for some way to get rid of Jesus, for they were afraid of the people. Then Satan entered Judas, called Iscariot, one of the Twelve. And Judas went to the chief priests and the officers of the temple guard and discussed with them how he might betray Jesus. They were delighted and agreed to give him money. He consented, and watched for an opportunity to hand Jesus over to them when no crowd was present"** (Luke 22:1-6).

Satan threw the first punch during Holy Week, perhaps on Tuesday or Wednesday. Satan entered Judas and tempted him to betray Jesus. Judas went to see the chief priests and the leaders of the temple guard, the Jewish leaders. They offered Judas 30 pieces of silver to hand Jesus over to them. Judas accepted the offer, and Satan landed his first punch.

Satan's second punch was thrown on Friday morning of Holy Week, just after Jesus was condemned by the Jewish religious leaders and led away to go on trial before Governor Pontius Pilate: **"When Judas, who had betrayed him, saw that Jesus was condemned, he was seized with remorse and returned the thirty pieces of silver to the chief priests and the elders. 'I have sinned,' he said, 'for I have betrayed innocent blood.' 'What is that to us?' they replied. 'That's your responsibility.' So Judas threw the money into the temple and left. Then he went away and hanged himself"** (Matthew 27:1-5).

Can't you just imagine Satan whispering in Judas' mind: "You betrayed Jesus even though you know he's innocent. Why did you do something so despicable? For the last three years you've been with him, seen his miracles, and enjoyed his teaching. Why did you betray him? You know the 30 pieces of silver you have in your pocket are blood money, don't you? You're no friend of Jesus. What must he think about you? He must hate you. You're a traitor. You don't deserve to live another day."

Satan's second punch landed a crushing blow. Judas saw no hope and no future and no reason to live. He returned to the temple, threw the money on the temple floor, and then went away and hanged himself. Satan's accusations led Judas to despair, then to his own self-destruction.

So what is to prevent us from ending up like Judas? If we try to ward off Satan's temptations and accusations by ourselves, we may indeed end up like Judas. The only way not to be knocked out by Satan's one-two punch is to have Jesus defend us.

**The only way not to be knocked out by Satan's one-two punch is to have Jesus defend us.**

There's a story in the Old Testament that symbolically foretells how Jesus intercedes and defends us against the relentless attacks of Satan. The story is a vision that the Old Testament prophet Zechariah experienced. Zechariah lived about five hundred years before Jesus was born.

The opening scene in this vision, recorded in Zechariah chapter 3, pictures three individuals standing near each other. First there's Joshua, who served as the high priest in Judah. He stands before the angel of the Lord. To Joshua's right stands Satan. The image is that of a courtroom. The angel of the Lord is the judge (and as we will soon see, also Joshua's defense attorney). Satan is the prosecuting attorney, and Joshua is the accused.

The word Lord (when it appears in the biblical text typed in small caps) is the name for God that emphasizes his grace. When God was about to give Moses the two stone tablets on which he had written the Ten Commandments for the second time, Moses declared the praises of who the Lord is and what he has done. Moses proclaimed: **"The Lord, the Lord, the compassionate and gracious God, slow to anger, abounding in love and faithfulness, maintaining love to thousands, and forgiving wickedness, rebellion and sin"** (Exodus 34:6,7).

The phrase "angel of the Lord" occurs more than 40 times in the Old Testament. Most often the angel of the Lord is the appearance of the preincarnate Son of God, which seems to be the case here. Other times in the Old Testament, the angel of the Lord appears as a representative of the Lord. Either way, the angel of the Lord is a visual appearance of the God of amazing grace.

Back to the courtroom scene . . . Satan accuses Joshua the high priest. We don't know what Satan says, but we are told that Joshua is wearing filthy clothes symbolic of the fact that, even as high priest, Joshua is an unholy man unqualified to stand in the presence of the holy God. In response to Satan's accusations, the Lord says, **"The Lord rebuke you, Satan! The Lord, who has chosen Jerusalem, rebuke you!"** (Zechariah 3:2). Then **"the angel said to those who were standing before him, 'Take off his filthy clothes.' Then he said to Joshua, 'See, I have taken away your sin, and I will put fine garments on you'"** (verse 4).

The angel of the Lord defends Joshua before Satan and declares that his sin has been taken away. He now wears what the prophet Isaiah calls a **"robe of his righteousness"** (Isaiah 61:10). Satan now has no case. He has no grounds for bringing any accusation against Joshua because the angel of the Lord interceded, defended, and declared Joshua free from sin. That's what God's grace does.

Also in this courtroom scene are seated Joshua's fellow priests. The angel of the LORD goes on to address everyone: **"'Listen, High Priest Joshua, you and your associates seated before you, who are men symbolic of things to come: I am going to bring my servant, the Branch. See, the stone I have set in front of Joshua! There are seven eyes on that one stone, and I will engrave an inscription on it,' says the LORD Almighty, 'and I will remove the sin of this land in a single day'"** (Zechariah 3:8,9).

Joshua and the other priests are a preview of the Great High Priest who was yet to come—Jesus, the Christ. Jesus would make his own personal sacrifice to take away the sin of the world.

Jesus is our High Priest. He intercedes for us. He defends us. He has declared us forgiven. And he has given us a robe of his righteousness to wear. The writer to the Hebrews sums up the work and the result of Jesus being our High Priest: **"Now there have been many of those priests, since death prevented them from continuing in office; but because Jesus lives forever, he has a permanent priesthood. Therefore he is able to save completely those who come to God through him, because he always lives to intercede for them"** (Hebrews 7:23-25).

Give Satan the credit he is due. He is a skilled accuser, a successful prosecuting attorney, who brings charges against us for having disobeyed God.

When he brings his accusations, call on your defense attorney—Jesus, our Great High Priest. What a blessing to have Jesus as our rescuer from sin's consequences and as our advocate who defends us against Satan's temptations and accusations.

# Conclusion

Satan isn't getting a lot of attention these days and even less respect. He likes it that way. Like a stealth fighter-jet pilot, he prefers to fly below the radar to unleash his attacks on people, especially Christians.

Like it or not, we are in a war. It's a spiritual war. **"For our struggle is not against flesh and blood, but against the rulers, against the authorities, against the powers of this dark world and against the spiritual forces of evil in the heavenly realms"** (Ephesians 6:12). The real enemy isn't a terrorist with an IED in his backpack or a military general with his finger on the missile launch button or a streetwise gangbanger with a gun in one hand and a knife in the other. Our real struggle isn't against flesh and blood. Our struggle is against the spiritual forces of evil led by Satan.

One of the most sobering facts about life is that all of us have a supernatural enemy whose aim is to keep us blind to Christ, ignorant of God's truth, and miserable in our own failures, and to do so by any and every means possible. Satan is our enemy, and we are at war with him. It's time to take him seriously and give him the credit he is due.

You might not want to be in this war, but you are. You might wish to sit this war out, but you can't. Everyone is in the war, and there is no neutral zone to escape to. There are two sides in this war. One either serves on the side of Satan or on the side of Jesus.

Although the war goes on, the enemy, Satan, has

already been defeated. The war has been won. Jesus himself defeated Satan. He resisted every temptation. He served as our High Priest, offering himself as the perfect sacrifice. His sacrifice on the Good Friday cross was full payment for the justice God demanded in order to save us. He rose from the dead three days later on Easter Sunday to declare his victory over sin, Satan, and death. The war goes on, but the victory has already been secured.

**Although the war goes on, the enemy, Satan, has already been defeated.**

In 1529 the reformer Dr. Martin Luther wrote a song about Jesus' victory over Satan entitled, "A Mighty Fortress Is Our God." The hymn beautifully summarizes Jesus' victory over Satan:

> A mighty fortress is our God,
> A trusty shield and weapon;
> He helps us free from ev'ry need
> That has us now o'ertaken.
> The old evil foe
> Now means deadly woe;
> Deep guile and great might
> Are his dread arms in fight;
> On earth is not his equal.
>
> With might of ours can naught be done;
> Soon were our loss effected.
> But for us fights the valiant one
> Whom God himself elected.
> You ask, "Who is this?"

Jesus Christ it is,
The almighty Lord.
And there's no other God;
He holds the field forever.

Though devils all the world should fill,
All eager to devour us,
We tremble not, we fear no ill;
They shall not overpow'r us.
This world's prince may still
Scowl fierce as he will,
He can harm us none.
He's judged; the deed is done!
One little word can fell him.

The Word they still shall let remain,
Nor any thanks have for it;
He's by our side upon the plain
With his good gifts and Spirit.
And do what they will—
Hate, steal, hurt, or kill—
Though all may be gone,
Our victory is won;
The kingdom's ours forever!

Give God the credit and the glory he deserves. Because of Jesus' life, death, and resurrection, Satan is judged. He can't harm us! Our victory is won! Christ's kingdom is ours!

Forever!

# Notes

[1] Jennifer Senior, "In Conversation: Antonin Scalia," *New York Magazine*, October 6, 2013, http://nymag.com/news/features/antonin-scalia-2013-10/.

[2] Barna Group, "Most American Christians Do Not Believe That Satan or the Holy Spirit Exist," April 13, 2009, https://www.barna.com/research/most-american-christians-do-not-believe-that-satan-or-the-holy-spirit-exist/.

[3] R. C. Sproul, "Satan the Proud and Powerful (Part 1)," August 12, 2001, www.ligonier.org/blog/satan-proud-and-powerful-part-1/.

[4] https://www.goodreads.com/quotes/122821-whenever-we-find-that-our-religious-life-is-making us.

[5] Tim Worstall, "Astonishing Numbers: America's Poor Still Live Better Than Most of the Rest of Humanity," *Forbes Magazine*, June 1, 2013, https://www.forbes.com/sites/timworstall/2013/06/01/astonishing-numbers-americas-poor-still-live-better-than-most-of-the-rest-of-humanity/#4a07e5e54ef0.

[6] https://www.goodreads.com/quotes/35282-he-the-devil-always-sends-errors-into-the-world-in.

# About the Writer

**Dr. Bruce Becker** currently serves as the executive vice president for Time of Grace. He is also a respected and well-known church consultant, presenter, advisor, and author. He has served as lead pastor of two congregations; as a member of several boards; and on many commissions, committees, and task forces. In 2012 he completed his professional doctorate in leadership and ministry management. Bruce and his wife, Linda, live in Jackson, Wisconsin.

# About Time of Grace

Time of Grace is for people who want more growth and less struggle in their spiritual walk. The timeless truth of God's Word is delivered through television, print, and digital media with millions of content engagements each month. We connect people to God's grace so they know they are loved and forgiven and so they can start living in the freedom they've always wanted.

To discover more, please visit timeofgrace.org, download our free app at timeofgrace.org/app, or call 800.661.3311.

# Help share God's message of grace!

Every gift you give helps Time of Grace reach people around the world with the good news of Jesus. Your generosity and prayer support take the gospel of grace to others through our ministry outreach and help them find the restart with Jesus they need.

**Give today at timeofgrace.org/give or by calling 800.661.3311.**

Thank you!

Finished 10-31-21